SCHIRMER'S LIBRARY OF MUSICAL CLASSICS

Vol. 623

D0504048

LUDWIG VAN BEETHOVEN

Op. 37

Concerto No. III

For the Piano

Provided with Fingering, and with a
Complete Arrangement, for Piano,
of the Orchestral Accompaniment

by

FRANZ KULLAK

The Introduction and Notes
translated from the German

by

DR. THEODORE BAKER

G. SCHIRMER, Inc.

DISTRIBUTED BY

7777 W. BLUEMOUND RD. P.O. BOX 13819 MILWAUKEE, WI 53213

Notes to Beethoven's Concerto in C minor

By FRANZ KULLAK

Our readings for the pianoforte-part of the Third Concerto are based on an edition published by Steiner et Comp. (No. 4029)*. This edition, except one newly engraved plate**, is to be regarded as an impression from the original plates, which thereafter (as we think we have established by a comparison with the original impression of the "Bureau d'Arts et d'Industrie") underwent no further correction.

Of the two versions of this edition, we have taken into consideration only the one which is accommodated to the extension (in 1804) of the pianoforte upwards to c^4. We have retained no distinctions in the staccato (' or '), having been unable to discover any consistent plan in their employment.

The arrangement of the orchestral accompaniment is based on Breitkopf & Härtel's score.

We were also enabled to collate the original manuscript score, in which, however, the piano-part still appears (in places) in a simpler form, and is not in all cases completely written out. But later additions and sketches (compare sketch on the last page) frequently permit us to recognize the present form. (*Cf.* Thayer, "Beethoven's Leben," Vol. II., p. 256.)

The parentheses () indicate an addition, or, in the Tutti, that different expression-marks are extant ; the brackets [ ] annul any sign enclosed in them.

---

* Full title : "*Grand Concerto / pour le / Pianoforte / 2 Violons, Alto, 2 Flûtes, 2 Hautbois, 2 Clarinettes, 2 Cors, / 2 Bassons, 2 "rompettes et Timbales, Violoncelle et Basse / composée* [?] *et dédié / À Son Altesse Royale Monseigneur le Prince / Louis Ferdinand de Prusse / par / Louis van Beethoven / Op. 37. / (Propriété des Éditeurs).*

No. 4029 .... *Pr. f 6—C. M. /*
À Vienne chez S. A. Steiner et Comp."

(Inside) "*S. u. C. 4029. H.*"—The old register No. 289 can still be readily made out in several places, beneath the new one.—The title of the original edition was precisely similar, except, at the end, "[No.] *289* [Price] *4 f 30 x^t. A Vienne au Bureau d'Arts et d'Industrie.*" It appears that Steiner & Comp., in 1823, purchased of the Industrie Comptoir their rights in Beethoven's works, either entirely or in part. We have also seen the following

Steiner editions : No. 4013 (song, "Sehnsucht") [No. 631 of the Ind. Compt.] ; No. 4032 (op. 56) [583] ; No. 4047 (op. 33) [171] ; No. 4054 (Variations on "Rule, Britannia") [406]; finally, the Fourth Concerto, op. 58, "*Vienna bei Tob. Haslinger No. 4031*" (inside : "*S. u. C. 4031. H.*"), formerly No. 592 of the Ind. Compt.

** This new plate begins with measure 10 on p. 35 of our edition, and comprises 38 measures. It contains some easily recognizable errors of engraving.—Other deviations from the original impression have been corrected in accord with said impression, and noted in the proper places.—The Steiner edition dates, presumably, from the year 1823. Compare Nottebohm's Thematic Catalogue, Second Edition, op. 114 and 121a.

Third Concerto.

Dedicated to H.R.H. Prince Louis Ferdinand of Prussia.

Composed 1800, First (?) publicly performed, and played by the composer, on April 5, 1803.   Published, Vienna, in the Bureau d' Arts et d'Industrie (1804).

L. van BEETHOVEN Op.37.
New revised edition, 1882.

Allegro con brio. (M.M. ♩=138; acc. to Czerny (1) ♩=144.)

(1) Carl Czerny: "Die Kunst des Vortrags." Supplement to the Great Pianoforte-Method, op.500.
(2) C (not ¢), in agreement with the original manuscript score in the Royal Library, Berlin.

Printed in the U.S.A.

(1) The Third instead of the Tenth, to facilitate playing.

(1) Facilitation:

However, according to Czerny, the last three chords should be arpeggio'd: this would render our transposition superfluous. On the execution of the trill, *cf.* Introduction to op. 15.

(1) The Tutti on the upper staves are sometimes facilitions of, and sometimes supplementary to, the lower arrangement.

(1) In the edition which we follow, the expression-marks for Tutti and Solo are of the same size. Although we do not hold espression-marks in the Tutti to be binding for Solo-entrances unprovided with expression-marks (either in the original or in our own edition), we have, nevertheless, to aid the player's judgment in certain passages, added the old marks, where they seemed doubtful, in [ ]; and marks borrowed from the score, in ( ). Also *cf.* pp. **23**, **35**, and (for this passage in particular) p. **60**.
(2) "Senza sordino" with pedal; "con sordino" without pedal (✳).
(3) Should it be *sf* ? See p. **15**.

(1) In agreement with the original manuscript score. *Cf.* the parallel passage, p. 17.

(2)

9

(1) ? See page 20.

15357

(1) Acc. to the parallel passage on p. 5. "*p.*"

(1) Only f♯, if the parallel passage were followed. The original manuscript score, too, has only f♯; in the left hand, rather in-
distinctly, (d, or c?).

21

(1) For Cadenza by Beethoven, see Appendix.
(2) See Note on use of pedal, in the Largo, p. 23.

(1) These 4 *sf's* belong to the *middle* notes of their respective groups.

Largo. (M.M. ♪=69; Czerny = 66.)

senza sordino (1) *e pianissimo.*

(1) "Beethoven," says Czerny, "who played this concerto in 1803 in public, held the pedal down through the entire theme, which did very well on the weaksounding pianos of the time, more especially when the soft pedal was also taken. But now that the tone has become far stronger, we should advise taking the loud pedal anew at each important change of harmony, but without causing any audible break in the sound." Our modern pianos require yet greater reserve.

(2) Reads as follows in the Steiner edition, which is, however, frequently incorrect in this movement in the matter of division:

It would be more easily intelligible thus: The ordinary emendation reads: Czerny gives: For a sketch from the autograph, see p.60. (3) Facilitation:

(1) Note added to replace omitted bass part.

28

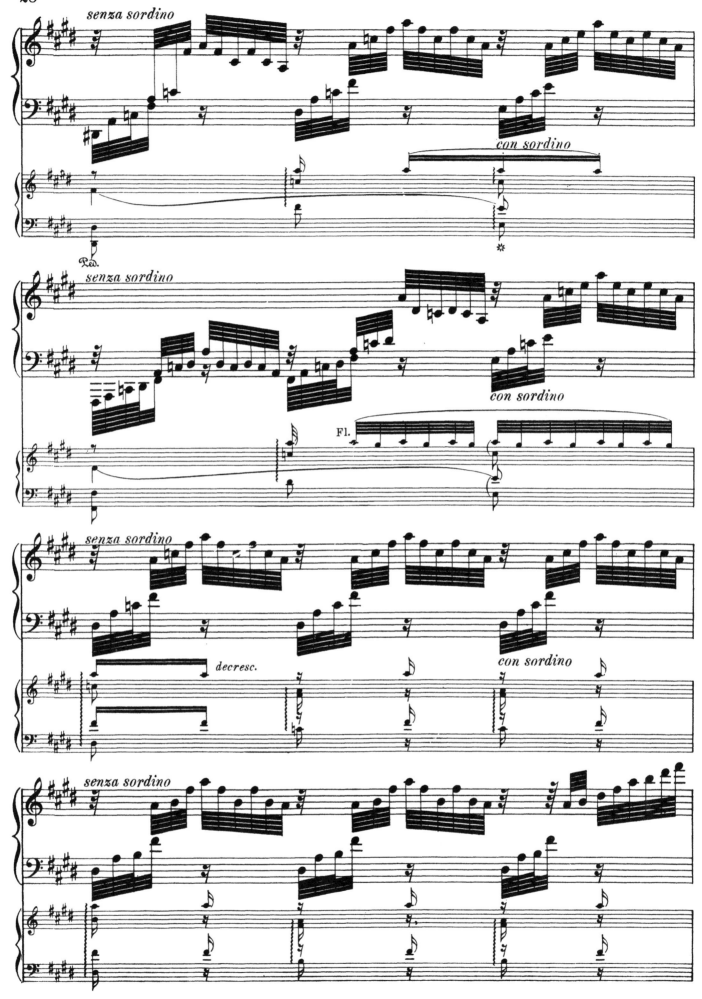

(1) Slurs belong only to the *3*.
(2) Here the same reading as above.

(1) The edition which we follow gives this *g* as an eighth-note. True, the following figure has a note-bar too few, but the notes are similarly placed over each other.___Other editions correct *g* to a 16th-note.

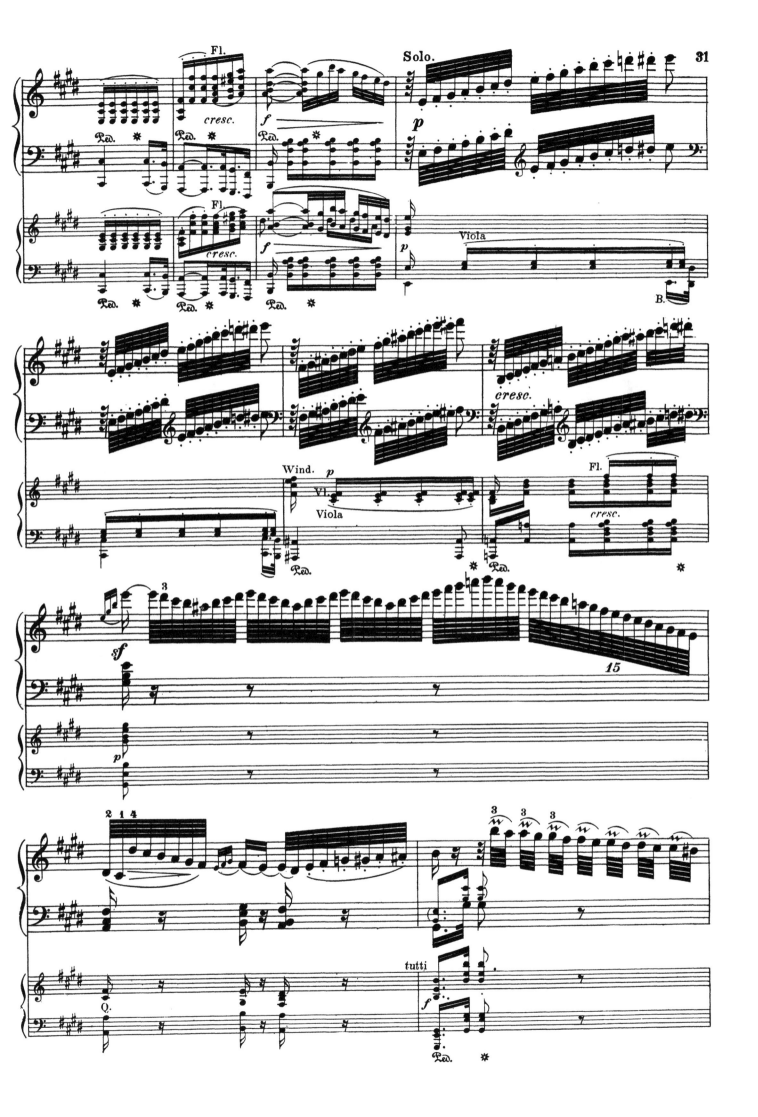

(1) In the original edition the *tr* is doubled (written above and below the *b*); perhaps one of these signs was intended to be an *f* or *sf*.

(2) Probably an engraver's mistake, in the Steiner edition, to make a♯–b eighth-notes; similarly, just before the hold to give the back turn in *large* note-heads.

(3) After the arrangement of the original manuscript score; but the Cadenza given in the latter had not assumed its present form.

Rondo.

Allegro. (M.M. ♩= 108; Czerny omits.)
Solo.

(1) Czerny adds **p**.

(1) If this *f* were to continue in force, it would extend through **44** measures. In the parallel passage on p.48, *ff* is given both times.
(2) One of these slurs was prolonged to the next-following eighth-note (see the parallel passage). Execution probably the same in either case.

(1) Acc. to the parallel passage, *sf* Slur also wanting.

(1) Facilitation:

(1) According to the analogous passage on p. 47, *g;* in the Steiner edition the note may have been corrected by the composer from *g*. In these two cases the orchestral accompaniment differs. The Autograph leaves the matter in doubt.

46

(1) In the Autograph the first *p* is rather indistinct. Perhaps the copyist read only *p*.

(1) Here *g* (*cf.* page 39).

48

(1) In the original impression, 14 of these slurs are prolonged to the eighth-note. (In the new plates, still more.)

(1) In the new plates, *sf* is omitted.

52

(1) The direction "*pp*" would appear to be anulled with the termination of the **Cadenza**. *Cf.* the orchestral accompaniment.

(1) A repeated ♯ (instead of ♮), both in the Autograph and the Steiner edition, is rectified by the orchestral accompaniment.

(1) Steiner gives the ♯ here, too.

(2) The words "con sordino" and "senza sordino" seem to have been interchanged; or else a preceding "senza sordino" was omitted.

(1) Facilitation:

Appendix.

Cadenza to the First Movement. (1)

Poco meno allegro e risoluto.

(1) This Cadenza was first published, as far as we know, by Breitkopf & Härtel in their Complete Edition of Beethoven's works, about 1861–63. Nottebohm's Thematic Catalogue of 1868 affords no information concerning the whereabouts of the Autograph; but says that the autographs of Beethoven's Cadenzas fo his other Pianoforte-concertos are in the possession of Breitkopf & Härtel. — Among Fischhof's literary remains (Royal Library, Berlin) we find *copies* of Beethoven's Cadenzas to his original pianoforte-concertos only to the op. 15, 19 and 58.

(1) Acc. to Czerny, Pianoforte-Method, Part I, such a trill may be played as follows:

It appears, however, that Beethoven did not leave out trill-tones in this manner; this is shown by a manuscript elucidation of a trill in Sonata 53. (Given in Thayer's Chronological Catalogue, p. 53.)

Soli and Tutti in the original impression.

(To page 5.)

etc.

The bass part (also, on p. 46 of the Rondo, the viola-part and an [incorrect] oboe-note) is written with large note-heads. Hence it might appear as if it had been executed with the rest in performance (*cf.* particularly the *Largo*). According to present custom, single bass notes coinciding with the solo would have a disturbing influence. We have, therefore, written them in [ ]. In the Autograph, in which the Tutti is omitted in the piano-part, we find, moreover, the chord

at the place marked *; and, in the following solo, only *c♭*, which, for evident reasons, is set an octave lower.

A Passage from the Autograph.

(To page 23.)

(The smaller notes are written in darker ink.)